Cowboys and Indians

Characters in Oil and Bronze

Cowboys

Characters in Oil and Bronze

and Indians

By Joe Beeler

UNIVERSITY OF OKLAHOMA PRESS : NORMAN

LIBRARY OF CONGRESS CATALOG CARD NUMBER: 67–24616

Copyright 1967 by the University of Oklahoma Press, Publishing Division of the University. Composed and printed at Norman, Oklahoma, U.S.A., by the University of Oklahoma Press. First edition.

To my wife, Sharon

About Joe Beeler *By Joe De Yong*

About Joe Beeler *By Joe De Yong*

Recognizing the qualities that may help to foretell the success of a beginning artist, like judging a race horse, follows no fixed rules. Talent and originality are obvious "musts"; but even with examples of the artist's work in plain sight, the deciding factors may never be apparent, since they are usually easily overlooked secondary qualities that ordinarily might be regarded as having little to do with art, such as personality, sensitiveness, fundamental honesty, and courage.

When chance first brought Joe Beeler and me together, he asked my opinion about his chances for success. My opinion, fortunately, was one that could be expressed willingly and with confidence. "In my judgment," I told him, "you have what it takes and will make the grade. While the first few years are bound to be rough in spots, you will come out on top." That opinion has happily proved true.

Joe has a breezy, pleasantly relaxed personality that imparts warmth to whatever he says or does. However, personality, ability, and training aside, his is a case in which fate seems to have taken a hand right from the start. His earliest recollections have to do with becoming an artist. Every seemingly accidental turn and twist in his life's trail has slanted in that direction, and instinct, judgment, and even blind luck have repeatedly proved dependable allies.

Of Indian descent—his father being part Cherokee—Joe is fortunate in having grown up among the Indian tribes of northeastern Oklahoma. It was a colorful, self-reliant way of life wherein horsemanship and hunting, particularly, served to provide a background that now supplies an inexhaustible fund of ideas for paintings, illustrations, and sculpture—at all of which he is equally gifted.

In addition, his hobbies are closely related to his work. The hobby in which he unquestionably takes the most interest is the collection of authentic old-time weapons of various kinds that have figured in the history of frontier America. Indian artifacts of the Plains tribes—on which he is something of an authority—and early-day horse gear hold a place of almost equal importance. At the same time he participates in big-game hunting, pack trips, "Sunday roping," and the seasonal work of neighboring cow outfits.

vii

Indeed, his interests, activities, and enthusiasms are so interwoven that even his relaxation seldom represents any real loss of time. On a stormy day when the light proves wrong for painting, he will often scout the cloud-wrapped hills surrounding his home in northern Arizona. And at day's end, when the winter winds howl among the weirdly eroded, overhanging rock formations of the near-by canyon's rim, he can be found comfortably settled in a favorite blanket-draped armchair perusing an account of some long-gone frontier character's life. By this seemingly idle-minded means his interest in the people and the times which he has chosen as the subjects of his life's work is constantly being honed.

More than a method, more than a system, his way of life has been somehow stumbled upon and gradually developed rather than planned. Forged and tempered by the always subtle forces of chance, necessity, interest, and desire, this way of life appears to have included as its keystone the ability to "bring home the bacon"—a rare, extremely valuable, and always admirable trait that is never taught in any school. It will also leave behind a rich gift for future generations to admire. Some of that is shown in the following pages.

Preface

Many times I am asked, "Why do you paint the old West?" Maybe I can shed some light on this question here, at the beginning of this book. First, I feel that the subject chose me rather than my choosing it. I can't remember when I wasn't interested in the West and when I wasn't drawing or painting about it on something, even if it was only a cardboard box lid or the borders of my school papers. My love for art and for the West came to me as a package deal. An artist interprets what he sees and feels, and I have tried to do this.

Many of the subjects of the paintings included in this book, I obviously could not have seen firsthand or experienced. Others I have seen or experienced. Imagination is one of the artist's most important gifts. It allows him to put down for others to see and feel, not artistic and beautiful pictures alone, but factual or historic events. The artist, through talent and research, can do this honestly and with heart, without having to witness the event. He does have to keep in tune with his subject, however, and this means constantly looking and drawing and actually living and being a part of this way of life.

I am an American living in the twentieth century obsessed with our rich heritage and history. Even today, the West is the last stronghold of our rugged American individualism, where we can still find old customs and traditions being followed. The cowboy and the Indian are still colorful characters, and there are places in the West that are yet unspoiled. These are the things I want to record for my own pleasure and for coming generations.

The paintings, bronzes, and drawings in this book are only a part of my efforts thus far, and only the beginning, I hope, the Lord willing.

JOE BEELER

Sedona, Arizona
September 1, 1967

Contents

Oils in Color

"As long as I can remember, I have been drawing or painting something about the West."

The Elk Hunter, 1967

30 x 48 inches, *Collection of Phil Phillips*

Cold Day on the Trail, 1965

24 x 36 inches, *Collection of William Woodruff*

2

The Trail Boss, 1966

24 x 36 inches, *Collection of W. K. Roberts*

3

Starting the Day, 1967

20 x 30 inches, *Collection of the Artist*

4

Scattering the Riders, 1967

24 x 36 inches, *Collection of William Whitfield*

5

Almost Home, 1966

24 x 36 inches, *Collection of Harvey Branigar, Jr.*

Captured, 1966

30 x 48 inches, *Collection of the Artist*

Dawn Attack, 1967

24 x 36 inches, *Collection of the Artist*

8

The Paintings

"In selecting these paintings, I started off with the early trail-driving days, went on to the modern cattle industry, and then added the Indian subjects."

Red River Crossing, 1963

The early-day cowhand was a mixture of different sorts, but for the most part he was reckless, homeless, hard living, and hard drinking. Cowhands were men who knew and cared more about cattle and horses than anything else. Few ever accumulated very much in the way of material wealth during their lives, but most of them died rich in adventure and experience. Most cowhands owned little more than their own outfit or equipment, a saddle of their own choosing, rope, spurs, and maybe a six-gun; a few odds and ends of clothing and assorted valuables—maybe a gold watch, books, or a banjo and a bed roll. Usually the cowboy was at home wherever he threw his bed roll down.

Soon after the Civil War, cattle became in demand. People were home from the war gathering up loose ends, seeing what they had left, and trying to make a new start. Herds of longhorn cattle were soon assembled in South Texas, and the long drives to the railheads in Kansas and on up the trail to Colorado, Wyoming, and Montana started. This was the colorful, romantic era of the open range when the cowboy was to become an American legend.

The cowboy at this point might be compared with the Plains Indian during the pre-white era, before he had become degraded by white influence and reservation life. At this time the cowboy was pure cowboy—no influence from other ways of life. He dressed and lived by a code created by his own kind, formed and adapted to his own particular way of life.

The young puncher in my painting has stopped for a moment to look back at the long line of cattle and men crossing the river and winding its way up the dusty draw. The drive is only one day old, and he is already looking forward to the end of it and pay day, when he will ride into Dodge City or some other frontier town and whoop it up, maybe spending his entire earnings in a single night.

24x36 inches, Collection of John Pabst

9

Incident on the Drive, 1960

A trip up the trail from Texas to Montana could be a very eventful journey. The cowboys who followed these drives had a wide assortment of circumstances and adventures to deal with at different times.

The weather could play an important role, for rain and floods or dust and dry water holes could be disastrous. A swollen stream or river might have to be crossed, and since many cowhands could not even swim, it took courage to jump off into deep, swift water, depending on your pony to take you across. On the other hand, lack of water could cause the thirsty cattle to go wild or mad, and even in good weather there was always the danger of a stampede.

Not all dangers were from natural causes. White outlaws and Indians posed a constant threat. On the southern end of the trails in Texas, the Comanche and Kiowa Indians were at war constantly with the ranchers and settlers. They took a heavy toll in cattle and horses, trading them to the New Mexicans or *Comancheros* on the Staked Plains. In the North the newly found ranges and grass-covered plains were old hunting grounds for the Indians of that area. At first large herds of buffalo were still to be found, but they were not to last much longer. As the buffalo were killed off, the Indians depended more on butchering the "white man's buffalo," the longhorned steers and the other cattle being brought into this rich grassland.

In my painting, the fellow riding point ahead of the herd has discovered the remains of an earlier traveler on the trail, a victim of an Indian attack or ambush. He has stopped to survey the scene, pulling his coat back away from the handle of his six-gun for ready use. Who knows what lies ahead over the next ridge or around the next bend in the trail?

24x36 inches, Collection of John Justin

Winter on the Trail, 1965

A pleasant sunshiny day with a gentle breeze blowing across the tops of wildflowers and sweet grass and time to day-dream and wander could give the cowboy cause to envy no one. But whatever the weather —and it was not always warm and pleasant out on the prairie—his work was outdoors, and if there was a blizzard or mud up to a horse's knees, he still had to get the job done.

Rain and thunderstorms frightened cattle and often caused stampedes. Running full speed in the middle of the night on slippery and unfamiliar ground to head off a steer could be a dangerous way to make a living. Working cattle in a driving rainstorm, then coming into camp and squatting in the mud to eat supper and rolling up in wet blankets to go to sleep, and then laughing about it all—this just might lead you to think that the cowboy either liked his job or was good at making the best of bad situations. Along with being tough and durable he also had to have a fine sense of humor.

On the opposite page we see that an early snowstorm has caught the trail drive on the plains, just at the edge of the mountains. The biting cold has worked its way through the heavy clothing of the trail hands—their feet and hands are almost frozen. The riders have stopped to build a small fire from sagebrush or what dry sticks they can find, hoping that this temporary relief might last them until they can get to a permanent camp or find other shelter. While civilized man has mostly used his knowledge and talents to reign over the animal kingdom, the cowboy many times finds himself no better off than the horse he is riding or the cattle he is driving.

20x30 inches, Collection of Sanders H. Campbell

II

A Pause That Refreshes, 1963

Few cowhands ever saw the ocean, and I doubt that many ever won medals for swimming. But it would be hard to find even a fish who enjoys a lake or stream more than this puncher is enjoying his muddy tank.

After making it through the cold winter without freezing a hand or foot and making it through the rain and mud without the sniffles, he finally finds himself smack in the middle of summer. The sun will tan his face and neck, and his old saddle will need a good going over with some oil to hold together another year. When the last heavy rains have gone, the hot wind starts to blow; and soon, where the ground was slick or boggy, it is now dry as gunpowder and blowing in the wind. Yes, this is summertime in the Southwest.

On many of the big ranges the water holes or tanks are fenced and a trap built. During the roundup, particularly in rough or canyon country, many cattle will hide out and not be brought in. Salt or a little feed is put out for them at these traps. A cowboy then makes the rounds of the different traps looking for these old mossbacks that held out.

The trap itself is built by hanging a throat or chute built of lumber or poles to a crosspiece. It works like a gate: the cattle push through to the water lot, then the throat closes behind them, trapping them inside.

This rider has been checking the traps on a hot day, and at this one, the temptation has been too great to try to cool off. He has rolled him a smoke, taken off his clothes except for his hat, and sat down in the muddy but refreshing water. It isn't a mountain stream, but it feels plenty good. After the wind dries him off enough to get his outfit back on, he will gather up the cattle and start them off for the ranch. The hot dry wind will soon make him forget that he was ever wet, but it was nice while it lasted.

24x36 inches, Collection of Spencer Stewart

12

Range War, 1960

In the days of the open range, the cowboy's way of life had many virtues and also many faults. The West had a different code for living from the rest of the country and part of it still holds today. Fair play and honesty were common practices on the range; a man was accepted on his face value.

The old-time cowmen were strong willed, independent, and resourceful individuals. The law was oftentimes far away or nonexistent. When crimes were committed and the guilty party found, justice was carried out just the same, usually at the end of a rope. The same cowboy who practiced honesty and fair play, when given sufficient reason by his boss, might be called on to use a Winchester or Colt instead of a rope and horse for his working tools. The cowboy in those days was very loyal to the outfit he worked for, even to the point of fighting or killing, if he thought it was justified.

Cowboys were not all as handy with a six-gun as television and the movies might lead us to believe, and many did not carry a gun. Disputes were often settled with a six-gun, however, and if they were not wearing one, they probably knew where they could find one real quick. When serious trouble needed settling, the gun was the tool used. Any other weapon, such as a knife, was not considered cricket.

Such an incident was related to me by an uncle who had heard the tale from my great-grandfather, on whose ranch the incident occurred. My great-grandfather was a well-to-do pioneer cattleman in central Texas. The time must have been soon after the Civil War. The neighboring cattlemen had gathered on his ranch to divide cattle that had been collected. Some crooked dealings were discovered, and the guilty party took off at a gallop for my grandfather's ranch house. He was pursued by the cattleman who had been wronged. The fugitive ran into the house, finding refuge under a bed where my grandmother and a daughter were still in the bed. The cowboy came in, put his pistol under the bed and killed the man right there. Nothing more was ever done about it, for the dispute was settled then and there.

20x30 inches, Collection of John Justin

The Fugitive, 1959

Some of the cowboy's frolic at the finish of a cattle drive ended in conversation, usually with his Colt having the last word. Whether in innocence or guilt, many an outlaw's career started with bad whisky and a fast gun, and it too often ended at the noose end of a good rope.

Other lawless careers did not have such an unplanned beginning. No cowboy ever got rich just punching cows, at least not someone else's. So, many set out to start their own outfits with little other equipment than a long rope and a running iron and lots of nerve. Some, not taking to night work, chose to go in for fine horses—anyone's fine horses. With little overhead and good profit, this profit had to be deposited for safekeeping in the local bank (for there were dishonest people around). Unfortunately for the banks, these depositors soon found that the livestock business was too slow when compared to the banking business, so instead of making deposits, they were soon making withdrawals. Even less equipment was needed for this work—just a fast horse and a ready six-gun were all that were necessary.

It was a lonesome way of life, as you can see in this painting.

18x24 inches, Gilcrease Institute of American History and Art, Tulsa

Lookin' for a Soft Spot, 1963

The dress and gear used by the cowboy varied with the period and the country he rode in. Most of the tack from the western side of the Rockies was influenced by the Spanish and Mexican elements, and during the nineteenth century one glance at a cowpuncher and his rig would tell immediately where he was from. The other influence was from Texas. The Texan's dress and saddle differed from the others. He was plainer in his choice of clothing and didn't go for much silver in his rig, though he might carry a pearl- or ivory-handled six-gun.

The southwestern cowboy operated in a lot of brush country, so he wore heavy chaps and became known for quick and accurate handling of his short rope. This came from roping in the brush, where he usually got only one quick shot at a critter.

Nothing the cowboy wore now or earlier on either side of the Rockies would save the puncher in this painting from a painful landing. Relaxing for a moment to roll a smoke on a green colt can be a "prickly" situation.

24x36 inches, Collection of Dr. Doyle Bladon

Bringing in the Remuda, 1964

The material that the cowboy's lariat is made of has changed since the open-range days, but the rope remains an essential tool in the trade of a cowboy today.

At the time when the long riatas were used, it took an experienced dalley hand to handle a big calf or steer with this light-weight line. You might compare it to fishing for a very large fish using light-weight tackle—you have to know what you are doing or you can lose your catch and wreck your equipment.

Today, since the introduction of nylon for lariats, you don't have to worry much about breaking your rope. Nylon ropes have been broken, but it is seldom, and when it does happen, it is usually the result of the nylon's being worn out to begin with.

Probably the two most highly specialized skills that the cowboy acquired was riding a bucking horse and roping. All hands were not good at both, or maybe either, but everyone admired these two accomplishments.

The old-timer in this picture has studied the rope to a science, and he will soon prove it to one of these wild ponies by throwing his loop and bringing it tight up around its throat.

24x36 inches, Collection of Joe Ansley

16

A Close Call, 1963

There are some combinations which are not good together, like chocolate cake and dill pickles or maybe gunpowder and whisky—those never went together. But another bad combination is a green broke colt and a wild cow.

Oftentimes a full-grown cow will have to be doctored or looked at out on the range. The cowboys, in this case two of them, have to rope the animal to throw her on the ground. One gets the head and the other the two hind feet, and they stretch her out. A young horse has to be taught to log or pull. Some of them come by it naturally, but most of them have to be taught.

In my painting, the cowboy who is still mounted has headed the big cow. This was the big chance for his pardner to show off his horse-training ability and drive his little colt in close to pick up the two hind feet in preparation for throwing the critter. This, as you can see, was a mistake. Something happened, and in a split second the green bronk was bucking off toward home and the would-be victim is about to eat the overconfident horse trainer alive.

The cow has caught the head horse off balance, and the horse is scrambling to stay on its feet—if he doesn't, the ranch may be looking for a new hand soon.

24x36 inches, Collection of Graham Sterling

17

Branding the Black, 1965

"Gentle" was a word seldom heard around old-time cow camps. The country and times were tough, and it took tough men and animals to match them. Horses were expected to buck and punchers were expected to ride them. The cattle were wild and hard to manage, and it took tough, firm methods to handle both horses and cattle.

In modern times, chutes, corrals, and mechanical gadgets have been designed to take the chance out of handling animals and getting certain jobs done, like doctoring and branding. With these new inventions, fewer men can handle more cattle and operate a larger ranch. The old, colorful ways and methods are slipping away.

Back in the days before pick-up trucks, any good-sized ranch kept a full crew of cowboys. Now a large outfit may keep only a couple of men the year round, hiring extra hands for a short time during branding. In the old days when there might be several hundred head in the remuda, there wasn't time to hand-feed and pamper each colt as is done today. If a big colt had to be branded or worked, he might be forefooted, as I have shown in this painting. The Spaniards handed this method down and they still practice and use it to some extent today. Nothing will take the fight out of a wild one more than to be taken off his feet and busted this way.

20x30 inches, Collection of the Artist

18

A Quiet Day on the Windmill Ranch, 1966

This scene should illustrate something about the strength of a nylon rope. I know something about this, for I am the figure in the foreground about to receive a sprained wrist.

We were team-roping one afternoon as the guests of my friend Duane Miller on the Windmill Ranch near Sedona. Ed Wright and I had just busted loose after a big red steer. Ed made a fine catch on his head and I came in and picked up both hind feet. As Ed got off to tie, his horse stepped back over the rope. No matter how gentle a rope horse is, he will not tolerate a rope between his legs. When he felt it there, he left like the devil himself was after him, steer and all. I knew to drive to the opposite end of the rope and try to stop him with the weight of my horse and the steer. I did so, and it did stop him—for a moment anyway, until through the dust I saw him come in again, wilder than before, still dragging the poor steer, whose neck by this time must have been six or eight inches longer. He hit the slack rope while I was still trying to get things organized. I went one way, my saddle went another, and my horse went yet another. When the dust settled, there was equipment scattered for half a mile in all directions, but the nylon and the old steer were still in one piece.

Water Color, 19x28 inches, Collection of the Artist

Fall Morning, 1965

Each cowhand working for an outfit has his own private string of horses to ride and care for out of the main horse herd or remuda. The number depends on the size of the outfit and the country he has to cover.

In this number he will have a favorite, a horse who suits him fine that can work cattle and do just about every job on the ranch. But you can't ride the same horse every day, and when there's lots of work, you can't even ride the same horse *all* day. This means the others get their turn. In the rest of the bunch he will have one that he dreads to ride at all, a snorty kind of pony that is good if everything goes right, but if it doesn't, watch out. Each horse has his own personality, and the cowboy knows each one. Ole Blue is a big stout horse and can handle anything you can put on the end of a rope. Baldy is good in the rocks and is a good traveler and will watch a cow. Shorty isn't much for looks but is an all-round kind of horse and you know he won't let you down, no matter what you have to do. Chief is good, too; he can run and knows all the ins and outs of cow work, but he has a talent for knowing when you're off balance and you have to keep your eye on him.

This is a cold, crisp morning; the cowboy is lighting his smoke and going over the day's activities, looking ahead to figure which horse is best suited for the job. The horses are looking and wondering, too, which one will have to go to work and which will get to stay and chew on the new corral gate.

20x30 inches, Collection of the Artist

20

Free Advice, 1965

Cow horses aren't born broke and ready to do a day's work on. It takes years for a horse to develop into a good ranch horse, and some never make it. Many cowmen will tell you that a horse is almost "over the hill" before he really knows anything. Some horses you can break and they will never buck or pitch; others will do it all their lives and still be considered good cow horses—you just have to watch them and try never to give them the opportunity they are looking for.

To illustrate this point, take the case of Duane Miller, a friend of mine who operates one of the big outfits in northern Arizona and used to help put on an annual rodeo at Cottonwood. The rodeo was small, and there were not the funds to hire big rodeo stock contractors to bring in bucking stock and bulls. Local ranchers would furnish cows to ride and Duane would bring in his using horses. Most of his horses would buck—all they needed was a little encouragement. A flank cinch or some high spurring would turn the trick, and the cowboy making a ride on any of these would earn his money. The same horses would be taken back to the ranch and put back to work the next day as the saddle-horse string.

It has all started for this young buckskin and the cowboy with his hand and hair full of corral dust. So far, the buckskin is ahead. He is looking back over his shoulder wondering what bit of advice the old-timer is offering his adversary. He might be heard to say, "Yur spoilin him. Hey! if I wuz a few years younger, I'd show you how to set up there in the middle of him and show him who's the boss."

Soon, though, the little buckskin will be in the cowboy's string, and he will learn to head off a runaway steer or lean into the rope and pull when his master has roped a wild cow or a calf to brand.

20x30 inches, Collection of the Artist

21

Fall Roundup, 1965

Here in northern Arizona, the fall roundup means gathering the cattle out of the high country where they have been on the rich mountain grass and driving or shipping them to lower elevations for the winter. Fattened steers and calves are marketed and ranges restocked.

Where Forest Service permits are in use, the rancher usually has a dead line for moving his cattle from the forest. One reason for the time limit, in addition to the coming winter, is the hunting season. I have seen evidence that cattle have been shot, either deliberately or by mistake—it seems to me it would be difficult to mistake a 400-pound steer for a tom turkey. At any rate, the rancher is eager to have all of his livestock out of the woods before the invasion of the hunters.

It is a fine time of year to be outside. The mornings are cool and crisp in the high country and the campfire feels good. Your horse is fed and saddled before the first hints of sunrise. The cowboys visit around the fire taking the chill out of their heavy leather chaps and their bridle bits. You mount up as it becomes light enough to see, each rider heading towards his given territory to push all the cattle towards the "hold." After all the cattle are gathered and thrown in one bunch, they are headed towards the shipping pens.

At first the cattle try to run and scatter, feeling good from the months on strong grass, and the cool morning gives new life to both horses and cattle. But soon everything lines out, and the sound of bawling cattle is mixed with the rustle of the wind in the fall leaves and the tops of the tall pines.

At the lower elevation where the cattle will winter, the wind is warmer and the tall pines give way to the golden cottonwood trees, and all is made ready for the winter work ahead.

24x36 inches, Collection of William Woodruff

22

Thanks for the Rain, 1966

The cowman has many partners and associates in his business. Probably the first one that comes to mind is the banker. He is the fellow that loans the money and holds the mortgages. There may be other partners on whom he relies—a close friend, a brother, or other relative—and there is the tried and true foreman, his right-arm man. Then on down the line the long list of people who help make the wheels turn—the cowboys and fence builders, cooks, wranglers, horse breakers, and, in modern times, the veterinarian who plays such an important part in the cattle industry. But after the list is completed and the partners, associates, and friends who, along with the cowman himself, make up the team that produces our beef, there is one more partner.

This is the fellow who is responsible for the miracle of life itself—the one who makes the wind blow to scatter the seeds of grass that covers the prairies and then lets the rain soak the good earth and the sun bring it strength to produce grass for the grazing herds.

God himself is this silent partner, and the old-timer in this painting knows and understands that it isn't all the banker's money and blind luck that keeps his world turning. We can see that the earth is parched, the tanks are dry, and thirsty cattle can be heard in the distance bawling through dry throats—some may have already given up and are now only feasts for the coyotes and crows. The seasons have come and gone, but still no rain has come. Then one day when all seems lost, the dark clouds gather and the long blue curtains of approaching rain can be seen blocking out views of mountain ranges and the surrounding landmarks. "Thanks for the Rain" seems to be small pay for so much.

24x36 inches, Collection of Lee Reeder

Race for the Dinner Bell, 1963

Outdoorsmen like to eat. Haven't you noticed that on a picnic out in the woods or on a camping trip everything tastes better, it seems, than it did at home? The cowboy, a few years back, spent most of his time outside, and as you might guess, the cook was an important fellow to any outfit. There is no better eating than the food that comes out of those black skillets and dutch ovens around a cow camp. Sitting cross-legged with a pan full of beefsteak and beans, dutch oven biscuits, and a cup of black coffee is an experience everyone should be able to enjoy at least once in his life.

People today can hardly enjoy eating for fear of polluting their bodies with animal fats or calories. New reports are printed every day of some new findings about the fatal effects the foods we eat each day have on us. Each time we sit down to eat now, we feel as though we are taking poison in small doses. It reminds me of a friend who was trying hard to quit smoking after reading the reports of the dangers of cigarettes. They were about to scare him to death, he said, so he quit— *reading*, that is, not smoking.

The cowboy was a hard-working outdoorsman and still is today. After spending most of the daylight hours on the back of a horse, year in and year out, he does not run much danger of being overweight or having to diet. Getting enough to eat is the only concern. During roundup and on the trail, in the old days, the chuck wagon was the kitchen. A top cook was the prize possession of any outfit. Although most cooks were known for being cranky, a good one could get by with almost anything, for the men knew that there were plenty of bad cooks to take his place if he was fired or he quit.

24x36 inches, Collection of Phil Phillips

24

In the Corral, 1965

Just about everything having to do with the cowboy, his gear, and his work is related somewhere up the line to the Spaniards or Mexicans, for they either invented it or named it. They also could use it pretty well, too, and the *vaquero* is a good man to watch today in studying horse handling and roping.

This painting was done from scenes I witnessed and participated in while working a roundup on a ranch in Sonora, Mexico. A couple of other artist friends, John Hampton and Charlie Dye, and I were the guests of an American ranching in Mexico, George Douglas.

The fellow doing the roping was the foreman. He was the best fed and had the biggest mustache and did all the roping in the horse corral, catching each cowboy's mount for that day. He used a rawhide riata or "gut line," as it is sometimes called. Of the fifteen or so cowboys, all but one used the rawhide; the one exception had an old, worn nylon. I was amazed to see this fellow stand, what seemed to me, too far away and flip his little thin rope far off into one corner of the corral and reel in a horse caught cleanly around his throat. The Mexican hands were artists when it came to dalleying and handling cattle with these small rawhide ropes.

None of the horses looked too gentle and many were not. They were small and wiry and tough as a boot. These boys seemed to like a little "pitch" in their horses in the morning and delighted in putting on a little show when the opportunity presented itself. They were a light-hearted bunch to work with, and even though it became very cold during the roundup and they were dressed for sunny weather, they never lost their sense of humor.

20x30 inches, Collection of Philip C. Kidd, Jr.

25

Shade, 1965

Probably most anyone who has traveled through the Southwest during midsummer has witnessed such a scene as I have painted here.

There is not much shade to a telephone pole, so you know something about how hard up this pony and the panting jackrabbit at his feet are for some relief from the burning sun. In country such as this, where trees are few and it is hot and dry, you will find livestock seeking out whatever shade they can find. It might be a deserted building, a windmill, or maybe a highway sign or billboard.

In the hot afternoon the cattle will go to water, and if there happens to be an earthen tank or pond, they will wade far out into the water and stand there for hours drinking and finding relief from the heat and flies.

18x24 inches, Collection of Dean Krakel

26

Down to Winter Pasture, 1963

To an artist who enjoys painting men and animals in action, looking at an empty landscape is like seeing a stage set for a play without any actors to give it life.

On a hunting trip near the Grand Canyon one year, a friend and I hunted and camped in such an area. Its grassy flats and low rimrock showed signs of supporting large herds of cattle. This was high country where the pines and cedars came together, and snow would soon be covering all the vegetation. The cattle had been driven down to lower elevations to spend the winter in less severe weather.

We hunted and camped there for several days, and I watched the sun rise and set on this country. It was the perfect background for a painting I had wanted to do. I made a couple of sketches, looked at the country good and hard, and the accompanying painting is the result of my efforts.

24x36 inches, Collection of Walter Bimson

27

A Southwest Cowboy, 1964

The red rock country near my home of Sedona, Arizona, makes the finest picture and background material for any artist looking for the very best in Mother Nature's handiwork.

The red earth is covered by a variety of plants and foliage, ranging from piñon pine to the many varieties of cactus and shrubs. In the spring wildflowers crop out in every nook and cranny and the yuccas and Spanish daggers cover the flats. The tall agave or century plant is one of the most beautiful things growing in this area when it is in bloom. For generations, the Indians of Arizona have used these plants for both food and manufacturing material.

The mixture of the many greens and grays of the foliage and the assortment of tall, windswept monuments of red rock make this one of the most scenic areas in the entire United States.

This is the winter range for the many cow outfits in the red rock country. The cattle are gathered in the spring and driven up the trails over the rim to the high, plush grass country of the mountain meadows and parks. They spend the summer there, fattening up on the rich grass, and then are driven back down to the lower elevations before the snow flies.

The cow horses in this country have to be long winded and sure footed, and the cowboys who live here are still outdoor people. My painting shows one of these horses and one of these cowboys in the red rock country. The scene could be anywhere during the spring or summer.

20x30 inches, Collection of W. Waits Smith

28

Prairie Fire, 1964

A scene like this strikes fear in the heart of anyone who has experienced a prairie fire raging out of control. This cowhand is making a dash for safety or maybe for help, for he and all the animals who live on the prairie know you must get out of the path of the fire or be destroyed.

In the regions where the wild prairie hay and grasses lie matted and dry, any spark or fire left unattended can set off a disaster. These fires will burn off hundreds of square miles of range land, taking the farms and ranches in its path and any living thing that does not get out of the way.

In the old days the Indians would set the prairie on fire to destroy their enemies or just to spoil the hunting grounds of a traditional enemy.

It is interesting to note that while all mammals and other creatures that live on the prairie will flee in terror ahead of a fire, it turns out to be an eventful time for the hawks. They will come to the fire, for it gives them an easy opportunity to attack the fleeing animals that they prey on.

18x24 inches, Collection of Philip C. Kidd, Jr.

Cheyenne Horse Thieves, 1965

Horses meant wealth to the Plains Indian. They were used as a medium of exchange, and one could buy a wife with them or pay a debt. The number of horses owned by an individual decided his place of importance and wealth in his tribe.

Acquiring horses became the main concern of these people and gave purpose to warfare and their nomadic way of life. A great deal of honor and courage was attached to the ability of a warrior to slip into an enemy's camp, untie his horses while he slept near by, and get away without being discovered. The Pawnees were great believers in this line of work, and they still refer to one another as "pony stealer" or "horse thief."

By the late 1600's or early 1700's, the Plains Indians were introduced to the horse. The horse changed their whole way of life. Up until this point, hunting was done on foot, and a hunter killed whatever small game he could find. The horse allowed him to cover far reaches of area, finding and killing larger game such as buffalo. It made him a king and lord over his environment.

Few of the tribes ever practiced any scientific horse-breeding programs. A good horse was a top possession, but little care was given to raising horses in any controlled manner. The Comanches in the South and the Nez Percés in the North were renowned for having good horses and did seem to give consideration to the raising and breeding of their horse herds.

20x30 inches, Collection of Dr. John Hilsabeck

War Party, 1964

The famous Apache war chief, Geronimo, is shown here mounted on the right. He has been a favorite subject of my research for many years. I have traveled his trails, ridden with his people at San Carlos, and studied written accounts of him and those associated with him. He was crafty and ruthless in warfare and was a thorn in the side of our military in the Southwest for many years.

He was not a hereditary chief such as Mangas or Naiche. He won this honor on the battlefield. He was a medicine man, and it was said that he was particularly good with bullet wounds and other wounds suffered in battle. Geronimo was a sturdy individual himself considering the wounds he received during his many years of battle: shot in the right leg above the knee and carried the bullet until his death; shot through the left forearm; wounded in the right leg below the knee with a saber; wounded on top of the head with the butt of a musket; shot just below the outer corner of the left eye; shot in the left side and also shot in the back. You might say he was durable.

He had many followers among the hostiles located on the reservation at San Carlos and was instrumental in several outbreaks after the Apaches were located on their reservations at San Carlos and White Mountain. He led raiding parties into Mexico, dodging back and forth across the border. During the Geronimo campaign of 1885–86 some 35 fighting men encumbered with the care of 101 women and children fought and held out against 5,000 troops, 500 Indian scouts, and an unknown number of civilians. During that time they accounted for the deaths of 2 officers and 8 soldiers, 12 friendly White Mountain Apaches, 75 citizens of Arizona and New Mexico on record, and probably over 100 Mexicans. Their losses were six men killed, two boys and two women and one child, not one of whom was killed by regular troops.

Geronimo's fighting career came to an end when he surrendered to General Miles in Skeleton Canyon, Arizona, on September 4, 1886.

24x36 inches, Collection of Philip C. Kidd, Jr.

Planning the Attack, 1964

The Apaches were different in some respects from their northern cousins when it came to reasons for fighting. The Indians in the North had been fighting for their land, the right to the buffalo herds, and all the land that had been theirs for generations. The Apaches fought for plunder, choosing to attack victims who would furnish trade goods, ammunition, guns, food, or horses. Hit and run was their policy: don't fight unless you can win. When attacked, the warriors would scatter like a covey of quail, each Indian slipping through the rocks or brush in a different direction, to meet days later at some preplanned rendez-vous miles away.

20x30 inches, Collection of Walter Bimson

32

The Captive, 1963

A hostage was valuable property to the hostile Indians. Hostages were taken on raids in both the United States and Mexico. Young children and women were usually the victims, men seldom ever being taken as captives.

Hostages could be used as a persuader or means of barter should the hostiles become hard pressed by white soldiers. Many times the children were kept and brought up as their own and came to know nothing but Indian life, even becoming warriors or wives of warriors. In other cases, however, they might be used as servants and slaves.

A classic example of the former is Quanah Parker's mother. Cynthia Ann Parker was a white child captured by the Comanches. She grew up in the Quahadi band. She was taken as a wife by Nokoni, then the leader of the Quahadis. Their eldest son, Quanah, was born in 1845 and became the leader of the Quahadi band. Quanah led his band in the Battle of Adobe Walls, and after the surrender at Fort Sill became the first recognized leader of all the Comanches. He became a good citizen and was looked up to by both Indians and whites.

20x30 inches, Collection of Spencer Stewart

33

Preparing the Ambush, 1964

The Apache in his actions was much like his desert counterpart, the coyote. You can hear a coyote howling near or even see him for a moment, then he is gone, almost before your eyes. He will keep every bush, no matter how small, between him and you, and he will slip away where you would think it was impossible.

Apaches would choose a high point in a narrow canyon over-looking a well-used trail to strike from ambush. Here in small numbers they could attack a mule train or any victim they chose and make quick work of it. Apacheland was well suited for this type of warfare, and later, when they were being chased all over the Southwest by our military, it was the nature of the terrain which made it such a long, tough struggle. With the combination of this type of country to work in and their own uncanny endurance and physical ability, the Apaches had things their own way for a long time.

18x24 inches, Collection of Phil Phillips

34

Ridden Down, 1964

During the Apache hostilities the citizens of Arizona and New Mexico could either stay out of the way of the hostiles or travel in force. But the cowboy had work to do out alone and in country which the hostiles crossed at some time or another. Small ranches and line shacks were often targets of Apache raids, for the Indians knew there were always good horses around where there were cowboys. They also knew the cowboy was not always easy prey. He could ride and shoot and was used to looking out for himself, and, in some cases, was as much of an outlaw as the Apaches.

But during the 1880's in southern Arizona and southwestern New Mexico, many a cowboy went to bed at night sleeping with one eye open and his pistol in his hand and mighty careful of who walked up to his campfire.

The poor puncher in the painting has been caught in the open by a band of hostiles on the fight. He has been set afoot, and his only chance is his dusty old six-gun. An Apache may ride over him, but he will have had his say before it is all over.

18x24 inches, Collection of Raymond Anderson

35

Fate of the Captive, 1965

Indian warfare was cruel and deliberate. War was a game with many Indian peoples, and great honor and prestige came from taking part in raids and battles against the enemy.

By white standards, the Indians' way of fighting was savage and inhuman and oftentimes foolish. But the Indians were fighting the only way they knew how, and they were waging the type of war on the whites that they had been waging on one another for generations.

Many times these customs cost the Indians a battle. How he fought a battle was more important to the Plains Indian, in particular, than who won it. To show courage and valor was of prime importance, and instead of taking advantage of a situation in order to win the battle, he would occupy himself with using the opportunity to gain personal merit and honor.

There were cases where whites were hopelessly encircled and out-numbered, awaiting their fate at the hands of the Indians. Instead of sweeping down on the outnumbered party and finishing the job, the Indians might stop and have a dance or celebration or become pre-occupied with some ritual for several days, allowing the enemy a chance to escape or reinforcements to arrive. I believe that this factor plus the inability or reluctance of Indians to organize was a principal cause of their defeat. When they finally realized they could not fight soldiers in the same manner they had fought one another, it was too late.

In this painting a trooper has been captured by a band of Comanches and is awaiting his fate. As was the custom, a warrior who had suffered last at the hands of the soldiers or whites was allowed to strike the first blow. This warrior may have lost a relative in a previous battle or himself been wounded, and therefore is riding out to strike the trooper with his heavy leather quirt.

20x30 inches, Collection of Walter Bimson

36

Return in the Rain, 1967

Even after the Apaches were confined to their reservations at San Carlos and in the White Mountains of Arizona, the old way of life of raiding and plundering still beckoned to many. A secret meeting would take place among those organizing such a war party. Its leader was usually a die-hard renegade who had proven himself many times in battles with the Americans and the Mexicans.

Oftentimes these war parties would not be mounted, depending on stealing their mounts along the way. Others would start out mounted, slipping out unnoticed heading south towards the border to raid into Mexico. Mexico was the favorite territory for terrorizing by the Apaches; they found the area just a few hundred miles south of the Arizona–New Mexico line easy pickings for their hit-and-run tactics.

The painting on the opposite page is a gloomy one. The day is gray and cold, the rain-soaked warriors returning from an unsuccessful raid. When they started, there were seven warriors; they have left four dead behind. The leader in the foreground, cold and damp, is thinking about what he will tell the relatives of the fallen—he will say his medicine was bad, but that he will be successful next time. If they had succeeded and brought home many horses and mules and other provisions to divide, there would have been long days and nights of dancing and singing, but now there will be no celebration.

24x36 inches, Collection of the Artist

37

Unaware, 1963

"Soldiers of the Cross" was the title given to the ministers who chose to spread the gospel of Christianity on the wild frontier. And soldiers they were, for along with such regular duties as preaching, officiating at weddings, and conducting funerals, they might be called on to teach school, labor in the field beside the farmer, or ride a bronc or rope a steer or maybe even take up a rifle or six-gun to help drive outlaws or attacking Indians from a settlement.

Even while the southern Plains Indians were still at war, the white ministers braved death to visit remote camps of hostile Indians to try and teach them the ways of peace and of Christ. Many were successful, and through the efforts of these brave men, many hostile bands stayed at peace and tried to practice the preaching they had heard. But not all the missionaries were successful, and some returned from months of living with the wild Indians broken in spirit and in health.

In my painting *Unaware*, you can see the lone figure in the buggy driving down the dusty trail towards an Indian camp, armed only with his Bible and Faith. Unknown to him a war party of Comanches is watching his moves, wondering what the brave little man in the dark suit is doing so far from help and civilization.

30x40 inches, Collection of Spencer Stewart

38

Changing Ownership, 1960

The Comanches and their allies, the Kiowas, were the plague of the Southern Plains. Cattlemen in Texas during the period of the Civil War and the years just after took heavy losses in property and lives from raids by these hostile nomads. The Indians would lie in wait at some vantage point along the trail and jump the herd, driving off or killing the cowboys, then taking all or part of the cattle. They would also raid the outlying ranches and settlements, driving off livestock and seizing whatever else they wanted or could take with them.

The Comanches were not in the livestock business themselves, but they dealt with people who were, the *Comancheros*. These were a group of New Mexican native traders, mostly cutthroats and thieves, who would rendezvous with the Indians at some point on the Staked Plains. Here they would trade whisky, guns, and trinkets for the plunder the Indians had brought from the settlements. After the trading was done (and before the Indians had time to sober up), the cattle were driven by their new owners to the Spanish settlements in New Mexico, only recently become a territory of the United States.

Many Texas cowmen, on trips through that territory, would observe herds of cattle being held by the New Mexican *vaqueros* wearing their own Texas brands. Charles Goodnight, the famous cowman and plainsman, tried unsuccessfully for several years to put a stop to this trade. It came to an end only after the warring Indians were put on reservations, thus eliminating the source of trade goods for the *Comancheros*.

20x30 inches, Collection of John Justin

39

Comanche Trouble, 1965

Along with the thriving *Comanchero* trade on the Staked Plains, there was another reason for the Indians' interest in the Texans' beef. The buffalo was fast disappearing, his range being given up to the plow and the spotted cattle. The hide hunters were finishing up with the southern herds, and all game was fast becoming scarce.

For the Comanches, life had always been hunting and warfare and the excitement of the chase. The settlers and the ranchers and their livestock now furnished all of these things.

24x36 inches, Collection of James Witherspoon

40

Navaho Horse Thieves, 1965

The horse-hunting Navahos in the old Southwest made life difficult for both white and Indian neighbors. Of all the wrongs and crimes committed against the pioneer cowmen by Indians, the one incident that bothered rancher Charles Goodnight the most was when a band of Navahos raided him in New Mexico and killed and ate his favorite saddle horse. Indians liked horses for more than just transportation.

Today you can still see evidence of the importance the Navaho places on the possession of horses. On his reservation here in Arizona and New Mexico, the land is in need of rain most of the year. Much of the Navahos income is derived from cattle and sheep, and there is hardly enough grass for them, but still an Indian might own many more horses than he needs. The government has tried, with little success, to get the Indians to cut down on the horses they keep, but large bands of roaming horses continue to compete with the cattle and sheep for the grass and water. The Navahos still believe that horses are wealth.

20x30 inches, Collection of Walter S. Light

41

Going Visiting, 1964

The modern Navaho has made few changes in his life during the past hundred years. He is a most interesting and colorful American. Anyone who has traveled through the Southwest is aware of the fine weaving and silversmithing for which the Navaho is noted. The amount and quality of jewelry a Navaho might own or wear is still the measurement of wealth and prominence.

A Navaho's life seems to be uncomplicated by modern civilization. He still lives in a hogan built from materials at hand and the horse still furnishes him much of his transportation. He holds to many of his old customs and, in general, is the last old-time Indian left in the United States in significant numbers.

20x30 inches, Collection of Dr. H. H. Ninninger

Watching the Whirlwind, 1963

"Mother-in-law" and "dust devil" are terms used by the Navahos for the huge spiral whirlwinds that sweep across the hot sands of their reservation in northern Arizona and New Mexico. During the summer or spring you can stand on a point where you can see for miles and watch as many as half a dozen of these whirling about at one time. Many Indians believe that they are evil spirits caught up and going about creating some devilish business.

This could be true, for I observed a Navaho horseman leaving a trading post one day on a young or very spooky horse. He was packing the week's ration of groceries in a sack. A good-sized dust devil approached, whirling a bunch of tumbleweed directly under the frightened horse. It was too much for him, and he unloaded his Navaho rider and his groceries right there and bucked off over a hill. For that Navaho, there really was a devil spirit inside the whirlwind.

24x36 inches, Collection of William Schofield

43

Oklahoma Summertime, 1967

The war dance or fancy dance is considered an original Plains Indian dance. It was probably copied by the Indians from the mating dance of the prairie chicken and other birds and animals. All tribes had their own versions of war dancing, however, dating back before the Indians were on the Great Plains. But today the war dance, as we know it, is the dance most commonly performed in the Plains regions. It has much the same status as the feathered war bonnet, which has become the trade-mark or costume of Indians all over the country, whether or not it was traditionally part of their customs.

The most widely accepted social dances among Oklahoma Indians are the stomp and the 49 dance. The stomp dance originated with the southern and eastern Woodland tribes, such as the Shawnees, Cherokees, and Creeks. The 49 dance came up through the Plains Indians and is performed in areas where they hold their powwows. Both dances begin after the regular program of war dancing and contests is over. They start at maybe midnight and usually last all night.

20x30 inches, Collection of the Artist

44

The Bronzes

"I have completed several new bronzes . . . some of them are subjects I have painted, and it is exciting to re-create them in three dimensions."

Navaho, 1965, 14 inches high, 15 castings

45

Apache, 1966, 13 inches high, 15 castings

46

Sioux, 1967, 16 inches high, 15 castings

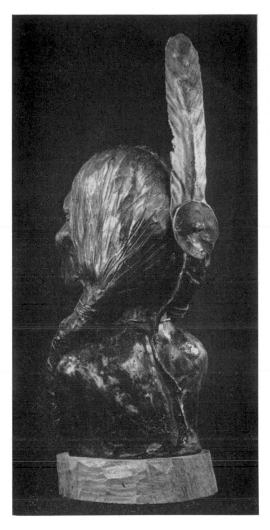

The Cowboy, 1967, 11 inches high, 30 castings

48

The Bandido, 1966, 7½ inches high, 7 castings

49

Widow Maker, 1967, 11 inches high, 15 castings

50

Longhorn, 1966, 5 inches high, 30 castings

A Joe Beeler Gallery

"This will not make up into one of those nice fat books with a lot of text—it is over half pictures, but the pictures are where I have done the most and best talking."

Old Whitehair, water color, 12x16 inches. *Collection of John Woodard*

Osage Man, ink and pencil, 11x14 inches. *Collection of Savoie Lottinville*

53

Sioux Chief, oil, 12x16 inches

Blackfoot Indian, water color and pencil, 11x14 inches

The Medicine Man, water color, 9½ x 12 inches

56

Navaho Man, water color, 10½ x 14 inches

57

Off to the Pow-wow, pen and ink, 10½ inches high

58

Tail Dance, 1952, lithograph (edition of 15), 11½ x 13½ inches

59

Cherokee Stomp Dance, pen and ink, 10x12 inches

Osage Straight Dancer, pen and ink, 10½ inches high

61

War Dancer, pen and ink, 10½ inches high

62

Fancy Dancer, pen and ink, 9x11 inches

63

Navaho, pen and ink, 8½ inches high

64

Apache, pen and ink, 5 inches high

65

Apache Scout, pen and ink, 10 inches high

66

The Trackers, pen and ink, 8x9 inches

67

Apache Cowboy (San Carlos, Arizona), pen and ink, 7½ inches high

68

Vaquero, pen and pencil, $4\frac{1}{2}$ x $7\frac{1}{2}$ inches

Cowboy with a Chew, pen and ink, 6 inches high

70

Ranch Hands Waitin' for the Irons to Heat, pen and ink, 10x12 inches

71

Team Tying, pen and ink, 12x16 inches

The Brush Popper, pen and ink, 10x12 inches

73

A Happy Cowboy, pen and ink, 9½ inches high

74

Open Range Cowboy, pen and ink, $7\frac{1}{2}$ x 11 inches

75

Rodeo Cowboy, pen and ink, 11 inches high

76

Texas Longhorn Bull, pencil, 5½x10 inches

77

Indian Pony, pen and ink, 6 inches high

JOE BEELER

78

Apache Pony (San Carlos, Arizona), pen and ink, 9x11 inches

Tired Rope Horse, pen and ink, 7½x11 inches

Index

xvii